THE BULL OF MINOS

'The story of the heroic discoveries grips
him and communicates itself to his
readers, who must welcome a book both
scholarly and easy, painstaking and alive
. . . It is written for those who may not
have met the Greeks and their history
before.'—FREYA STARK in *Time and Tide*.

'Mr Cottrell has been fascinated by the
story of Schliemann's and Arthur Evans's
discoveries. He has not only passionately
studied the literature of Aegean archaeo-
logy, but he has visited most of the impor-
tant sites and conveys vividly his sense of
excitement and discovery.'
                    —*Manchester Guardian*.

'This book is a stimulating introduction
to the Mycenaean Age of Greece.'—SIR
JOHN FORSDYKE in *Sunday Times*.

Furthermore, after he (Theseus) was arrived in Creta, he slew there the Minotaur (as the most part of ancient authors do write) by the means and help of Ariadne; who being fallen in fancy with him, did give him a clue of thread, by the help whereof she taught him, how he might easily wind out the turnings and cranks of the Labyrinth.

Plutarch (North's translation).